KETTLEBELL TRAINING

Burn Fat and Get Lean and Shredded With Total Body Kettlebell Training

(The Fastest Way to Strength and Muscle)

Julie Madison

Published by Tomas Edwards

© **Julie Madison**

All Rights Reserved

Kettlebell Training: Burn Fat and Get Lean and Shredded With Total Body Kettlebell Training (The Fastest Way to Strength and Muscle)

ISBN 978-1-990268-60-1

All rights reserved. No part of this guide may be reproduced in any form without permission in writing from the publisher except in the case of brief quotations embodied in critical articles or reviews.

Legal & Disclaimer

The information contained in this book is not designed to replace or take the place of any form of medicine or professional medical advice. The information in this book has been provided for educational and entertainment purposes only.

The information contained in this book has been compiled from sources deemed reliable, and it is accurate to the best of the Author's knowledge; however, the Author cannot guarantee its accuracy and validity and cannot be held liable for any errors or omissions. Changes are periodically made to this book. You must consult your doctor or get professional medical advice before using any of the suggested remedies, techniques, or information in this book.

Upon using the information contained in this book, you agree to hold harmless the Author from and against any damages, costs, and expenses, including any legal fees potentially resulting from the application of any of the information provided by this guide. This disclaimer applies to any damages or injury caused by the use and application, whether directly or indirectly, of any advice or information presented, whether for breach of contract, tort, negligence, personal injury, criminal intent, or under any other cause of action.

You agree to accept all risks of using the information presented inside this book. You need to consult a professional medical practitioner in order to ensure you are both able and healthy enough to participate in this program.

Table of Contents

INTRODUCTION 1

CHAPTER 1: WORKOUT PRINCIPLES 3

CHAPTER 2: THE KETTLEBELL 7

CHAPTER 3: KETTLEBELLS AND FUNCTIONAL STRENGTH . 11

CHAPTER 4: FORCE MULTIPLIERS: THE 3 KEY MOVES THAT BENEFIT EVERYTHING 17

CHAPTER 5: BEFORE YOU START 27

CHAPTER 6: INTERMEDIATE EXERCISES 41

CHAPTER 7: WORKOUT ROUTINE 49

CHAPTER 8: FULL BODY OR HOLISTIC EXERCISES 57

CHAPTER 9: KETTLEBELL EXERCISES 64

CHAPTER 10: WORK OUTS 77

CHAPTER 11: WAYS TO USE KETTLEBELLS 99

CHAPTER 12: KETTLEBELL GOBLET SQUAT 102

CONCLUSION 112

Introduction

For many people, a shredded body is nothing but an impossible dream. Maybe they've tried all the diets and training programs in the world but have never achieved that low-enough level of body fat to expose those abs and crazy muscular detail for the shoulders, arms, chest and legs. And so they've let go of such a dream. Maybe you're one of them.

Chances are, the reason for their – or even your own – inability to achieve a shredded body is lack of continuous stimulation. With traditional training programs, it's possible that their or your muscles have already adapted to the stimulus. As such, progress has plateaued. The key therefore is to train differently in a way that stimulates the muscles in a whole new way – even those muscles that aren't stimulated with the usual weight training programs.

Enter kettlebell training. In this book, you'll learn how it can help you get ripped and shredded and, more importantly, how to start with the right set of kettlebells, i.e., the right quality and weight. By the end of this short book, you'll be in a great position to start going for that ripped and shredded body you've always dreamed of using kettlebells. You have a great tool in your hands now. It's up to you if you'll use it to the hilt.

If you're ready to shred your dream body, turn the page and let's begin!

Chapter 1: Workout Principles

There are no shortcuts to losing weight. You have to do your part to be able to achieve your dream body. The amount of work needed will vary depending on your current fitness status and your fitness goals.

Set your Goals

Every important achievement starts with a goal. It will be easier to accomplish your fitness achievement if you also start it with a goal. In stating our goals, we need to make sure that they are specific. It should not be open to any other interpretation. If you aim to lose weight, you should have a number of kilograms or pounds stated in your goal. If it is about having abs, you should measure the diameter of your tummy and you should look for a picture of a fit and toned abs to use as reference.

Your goal should also have a deadline, but make sure that it is realistic. Ensure that you can accomplish your goals according to the deadline that you set. Setting a deadline that is too near will leave you frustrated because you will not be able to reach your goals on time. Setting a deadline that is too far may also lead you to fail. People usually procrastinate when they have too much time to finish a goal.

Lastly, your fitness goals should be reachable based on your resources. You should make sure that you have access to all the things that you need to reach your goals.

People who start working out usually have two common goals in mind; to lose weight and to look good. You should stop and think after this chapter to assess what you want to achieve in getting into the kettlebell WOD program suggested by this book. You should put it into writing and paste it in a place where you will always see it.

Your additional goal:

Aside from your personal goals, it is the duty of every workout mentor to encourage you to keep a healthy lifestyle. After reaching the goals that you set today, you must set more goals to work for. If you continue to do this, you will be able to make your workouts a part of your lifestyle. By doing this, the fitness accomplishments that you achieve will become permanent. You will have a toned physique and an athletic frame even when you grow older. You will also be able to maintain a healthy weight even as you enter middle age. This is usually the time when people start failing to meet their scheduled workouts and start gaining weight and beer belly.

The Role of Nutrition

Though this book focuses on the workouts, it also teaches the role of nutrition in your weight loss and fitness goals. Just because you workout often doesn't mean that you can eat any type or amount of food that you like. We will discuss the best kind of diet that will best work with your high intensity workouts.

This will be discussed in the later parts of the book.

Chapter 2: The Kettlebell

The kettlebell, also known as a ball dumbbell, is, as the name implies, a dumbbell in a spherical shape. This ball usually has a flattened footprint that prevents the kettlebell from rolling away or makes it easier for you to balance when leaning on it while exercising. This is also the first point to keep in mind: If the ball dumbbell does not have this surface, this greatly limits the range of use, and you should better look for another one.

At the upper part of the ball dumbbell, a handle is attached, which can vary depending on the manufacturer for different lengths of relationship meadow. A wider grip allows you to grip the kettlebell more easily with both hands, while a narrower grip facilitates one-handed training, as the shorter grip reduces freedom of movement less. The decision whether you prefer a broader or a narrower grip is entirely up to your personal preference, and it just makes sense with increasing weight of the ball dumbbell to have a broader grip to be able to train with the dumbbell at all.

A high-quality dumbbell can be recognized by the fact that it is either made of 100% iron and may have a silicone or plastic coating, especially for indoor and home use, or consists of a plastic housing filled with sand or concrete. What you prefer is entirely up to you.

As well as a dumbbell and barbell, the kettlebell falls into the area of free strength training. This means that compared to fitness machines, your movements are not guided, so you have to pay more attention to proper movement, and your support muscles are trained with the same.

Proper weight training with the ball dumbbell

In contrast to pure fitness training, the weight or strength training is not only working with your body weight but with additional weights to promote muscle growth. The additional weights not only increase the training effect but also the risk of injury, so you should have a little before with the subject "free strength training" dealt with.

Above all, it is important that you have warmed up very well before the very muscle-strength training with the ball dumbbell. This makes the muscles and ligaments supple and, to some extent, stretchable, which greatly reduces the risk of ligament strains, muscle fiber or tears, and strains. Also, you should always pay attention to your movements: If a movement feels funny or even hurts, you are doing something wrong, and you should go through the sequence of movements again. Another positive effect of the result is that if you pay attention to the movement, you automatically slow down the movement. This makes it easier for your body to save the movement and at the same time, boosts the training effect.

Another tip: do not just fix the part you need for the movement, but also the rest of the body. This helps to prevent other parts of the body from becoming "cold" again and increases the stability of your body during training and thus additionally secures your movement.

Chapter 3: Kettlebells And Functional Strength

A recent focus in the fitness world is functional training. Functional training involves exercises that will prepare you to perform better in normal life routines, as well as over a range of sports and activities rather than focusing on one. Functional training is an integrative approach that seeks to use all parts of the body in a constructive way. To this end, functional training doesn't always target specific muscle groups, as in traditional bodybuilding for example, but instead recruits a large amount of muscles over the course of a single movement.

The health club style of training that has been popular over the past 30 or so years is a direct comparison to this functional, integrative approach to training. The health club approach, using Hammer Strength or Nautilus machines, would focus on single muscle groups and hypertrophy training. While this isn't an inherently bad way of training, and in fact can make for some fantastic results if your goal is mainly for looks, it doesn't create strength that is as at home in the martial arts gym, running track, yoga studio or backyard as it is in the gym.

One of the reasons for this is that training by targeting single muscle groups (like in a bodybuilding style program) can lead to unconsciously neglecting other muscles, while also forgoing mobility and flexibility as part of the overall regimen. Functional training takes all of these areas into consideration and looks to merge many conflicting parts into a unified whole. What can I do in the gym to make myself perform better at the Muay Thai gym and at indoor soccer on a Friday night and when I help my friend build a fence at his house on Saturday? Functional training seeks to answer these types of questions.

Kettlebells as functional training

Kettlebell training is a perfect example of a functional training plan. While there are times where you will target specific areas and muscle groups, such as with presses or squats, a complete workout and program will involve many different muscle groups and thus it will translate into more calories burned, more muscle growth and will allow you to effectively learn to use your body in other sports and disciplines.

An example movement is the swing. A simple momentum-based movement like the swing will incorporate the legs, lower back, glutes, core, shoulders and grip. One movement, yet total body function. The research also supports that the swing will burn calories at the same rate as some sorts of endurance training.

A compound movement like the double kettlebell thruster is another example of a full-body, functional exercise, and this squat-into-press movement build total body strength and power. All of the small movements that go into this larger movement will build strength and power across your entire body.

Another factor that leads to kettlebells being effective for building function strength is the shape and offset weight of the implement. Because of these factors, you can perform many more movements than with a barbell or with your bodyweight. Think of the muscle recruitment necessary for a workout consisting of kettlebell goblet squats, see-saw presses and swings. This is a simple workout, but it allows almost every muscle in the body to be used.

Kettlebells are, quite simply, the most effective implements for growing functional strength and power, especially if you limited space and a limited budget. Kettlebells are an incredible way to build strength through the entire body, especially with the core and with grip. Grip and core strength are two of the most important areas to target as they offer the most carry-over into real-life strength needs.

Stability and Mobility

One of the specific functional benefits of kettlebell training is how it builds stability and mobility - two cornerstones of functional fitness. Unlike a barbell, kettlebells allow you to use 1 arm or leg for movements yet unlike a dumbbell, the odd shape of a kettlebell creates an altogether different stimulus.

Mobility and stability are closely related and represent two sides of the same coin. Mobility is how flexible you are - how well you are able to move and achieve end range of motion in joints. Having good mobility will mean that you can bend down and touch your toes or get into a full squat position or rotate your shoulders overhead so that your biceps touch your ears, as examples. Stability is using your body to actively resist movement. An example of stability would be keeping a flat back while deadlifting or carry a weight in one arm and resisting the need to bend to that side.

Mobility and stability are very important markers of overall strength and health. Kettlebell training can assist in creating mobility and stability by simulating both within a single movement. Again, take a swing as an example. In one movement you are increasing mobility with the momentum of the swing while simultaneously resisting rounding your back - stability.

While the basic movements will increase mobility and stability, some of the more advanced movements, like the windmill, halo and get-up, will dramatically improve both your flexibility and ability to keep a health body shape while moving loads in compromised positions.

Chapter 4: Force Multipliers: The 3 Key Moves That Benefit Everything

Less is often more; the three moves below can rectify imbalances, improve athletic performance and improve your functional movement in all areas. We as humans seem to have a need for something to be complex before we think it will be effective. If you were to simply do each of the below exercises once a week you will be miles ahead of the "isolation exercises" crowd as it is impossible to complete any of the below three without hitting the majority of your muscles.

The kettlebell swing is great for working your posterior chain, abs, glutes and hamstrings. All are hard to hit muscle groups and ones that directly translate to your efficiency in both running and jumping. The kettlebell swing can be viewed as a less technical version of a deadlift, yet one that provides most of the benefits of deadlifting. An additional benefit of the swing is that a large proportion of people are quadriceps dominant, so performing swings can assist in balancing out the glutes and hamstrings which are often neglected in training.

Personally the Turkish Get-up is my least favourite exercise, but the one I find I derive the most benefit from as it teaches the whole body to work as one from head to toe. It is very useful for correcting weaknesses in certain planes of movement. To perform the exercise correctly requires a certain amount of flexibility and stability throughout a whole range of movements. Ensure you start off with a very light kettlebell until the movement can be completed without any catch points or unnecessary strain.

The last exercise is the squat and press, which should be the foundation of your training along with the other two exercises mentioned above. Aim to get as deep into the squat as possible for maximum benefit. On a side note, you should be able to sit on your heels comfortably without your heels leaving the floor. Unfortunately not many people have this flexibility, due mostly to chairs and toilets eliminating our ability to perform a deep squat. Ensure your back is straight throughout the entire movement and aim to execute each rep as explosively as possible to get the maximum benefit from it.

Kettlebell Swings

Great for developing strong glutes, hip flexors, quadriceps and shoulders.

Works the posterior chain helping to strengthen hamstrings, middle and lower back.

Fantastic for sports which require explosive movement i.e. sprinting and jumping.

For repetitions there are two ways to go about it either timed intervals i.e. 2minute intervals working up to 5minutes intervals to see how many repetitions you achieve for 3 sets. Or the alternative is to aim for 30 repetitions and 3 sets, progressing after 2-3 months to 40-50 reps should be achievable. The ultimate aim is to be able to complete a set equal to your body weight in kilograms, i.e. 1kg = 1 rep or 80kgs – 80 reps appears challenging I know, but is a great goal to work towards.

Keep your heels down and the weight from the mid-part of your foot back towards your heels. Lift your toes if your knees pitch forward.

Your arms should remain relaxed as they are simply the lever to transmit the power of the hip drive through the torso and into the kettlebell.

Pop your hips hard, the hip snap should drive the kettlebell explosively up.

Tip: Use a small towel to wrap around the handle and grip either side of the towel, as when starting out as this will ensure you don't use your arms in the movement and that it is all lower body drive from the hips.

Grasp the kettlebell with both hands in an over hand grip.

Stand upright with your feet slightly wider than shoulder width apart.

Lean forward at your waist and bend your knees, similar to the start of a squat.

With both hands on the kettlebell swing it back between your legs so your forearms are in your groin. Keep your abs tight.

Drive the kettlebell up with an explosive thrust forward with your hips, driving through your heels. At the same time your hips come forward, your torso rises and the kettlebell should move in an arc to roughly chin height.

Reverse the movement by pushing your hips back and letting your arms follow the same path back between your legs. Aim to hike the bell as far back behind you as you can before commencing the next rep.

Turkish Getups

Great for developing chest, glutes, hip flexors, hamstrings, abs, middle and lower back, lats

Quadriceps and shoulder. In other words, it pretty much works everything!

One of the best core exercises you can do - it's like an abdominal bridge on steroids.

Improves shoulder stability, mobility and strength as well as body control, awareness and coordination.

Great for identifying and correcting weak points in certain planes of movement, as your body must work as unit to complete the movement.

Aim for 5-10 (quality) reps each side for 3 sets. I highly recommend you YouTube the Turkish Getup, as the illustrations below do not capture the complexity of the movement.

Starting in the foetal position; grasp the kettlebell in your right hand and then roll onto your back. Bend in your right leg while keeping the left extended. Press the kettlebell into the air with your right hand until your arm is straight. Place your left hand on the ground.

Raise yourself up onto your left elbow. Now sit up, aiming to keep your arm straight with the kettlebell in the air. Drive your hips into the air. Bring your leg into a kneeling position. Rotate your back knee so that your body is in a lunge. Step forward and then stand up straight.

Squat Press

This should be your base exercise; a great compound move.

Use a weight in which you are able to do 15-20 reps for 3 sets or lower weights and use timed intervals, ensuring a great mix of strength and cardio training.

Focus on squatting deep to reach even more muscles.

Look to explode out of the squat pressing through your heels then the balls of your feet to help build your quick twitch muscle fibres.

Maintain a straight back at all times (Tip: always look up when at bottom of squat, as this helps to ensure that your back remains straight.)

Tense abs and squeeze your butt throughout the exercise especially from the squat position through to the top of the press.

Extending through the legs and hips, pull the kettlebells towards your shoulders, rotating your wrists as you do so. This will be your starting position.

Begin to squat by flexing your hips and knees, lowering your hips between your legs. Maintain an upright, straight back as you descend as low as you can.

At the bottom, reverse the direction and stand by extending your knees and hips while pushing down through your heels. As you do so, press both kettlebells overhead by extending your arms straight up, using the momentum from the squat to help drive the weights upward.

As you begin the next repetition, return the weights to the shoulders.

Chapter 5: Before You Start

It is vitally important to read this section before progressing to any of the exercises detailed in later chapters of this book. This chapter contains crucial information that everybody needs to know before they start with kettlebell exercises to ensure their health and safety while using this guide.

PROCEED WITH CAUTION

Before embarking on any new exercise journey, it is advisable to consult a medical practitioner. Only a qualified physician, or even a specialist, can recommend whether a specific fitness routine is suitable for you. Kettlebell exercises are no different. You can research your ideal starting weight, take a lesson from an instructor to perfect your form, and take every precaution possible to ensure safety while training. However, none of these sources of guidance can compare to expert medical knowledge. Your physician may not ax kettlebells altogether, after all they are an excellent form of exercise. However, they may recommend a lower starting weight or that you focus on specific exercises and steer clear of those that may cause injury specific to your personal health.

HEALTH CONDITIONS AND KETTLEBELLS

If you have any underlying medical conditions, you must seek medical advice before even picking up a kettlebell. Medical conditions may include, but are not limited to:

Health conditions such as diabetes, cardiovascular disease, hypertension, arthritis, or any other health concerns which you may or may not think will be affected

If you have had any form of joint, tendon, or muscle surgery or joint replacements recently or in the past

If you are suffering from any current injuries

If you have suffered any serious injury in the past, even if it has fully healed, a serious injury in the past can leave behind a weakness which could get re-injured

If you suffer from any temporary or chronic pain in any part of your body

AGE AND KETTLEBELLS

Kettlebells can form an excellent part of an effective fitness routine for any adult, regardless of their age. While age is generally not much of a consideration for younger fitness enthusiasts, more mature people wanting to start with kettlebells should seek medical advice before they start. There are many fit, healthy, and strong people of a more mature age. However, the risk of injury involved with taking up kettlebells as a form of fitness training, or any other exercise plan, could be higher or injuries more serious in older exercisers.

PREGNANCY AND KETTLEBELLS

Pregnancy is a beautiful part of a woman's life. Pregnancy can also be a time of anxiety for new mothers, those who have had problematic pregnancies before, or mothers who may have concerns about potential problems during their pregnancy. The question, therefore, becomes whether you can use kettlebells safely during pregnancy.

Never attempt a new form of exercise during pregnancy. If you weren't doing it before pregnancy, don't start now. There is good news in that many women can continue the fitness routine they enjoyed prior to pregnancy during their first two trimesters.

Always consult your obstetrician before continuing your exercise regime into pregnancy, even if you are expecting to have a typical, healthy pregnancy or have had a previous healthy pregnancy. Seeking expert advice is always advisable to ensure the health and safety of both mother and baby. You may be cautioned against certain exercises that seem harmless at first glance or you may be limited as to how far into your pregnancy you can continue particular exercises.

Once you have the go-ahead from your obstetrician, kettlebell workouts are a great way of maintaining fitness, health, and limiting the gain of baby weight during your pregnancy.

KNOW YOUR NUTRITION

Nutrition is a vital aspect of overall health and important when you are following a dedicated fitness plan that requires the correct fueling for optimum performance. Nutrition is even more important if you are trying to follow a fitness plan and burn fat at the same time. You cannot achieve your desired results if your nutrition isn't in line with your goals whether you want to lose weight, get toned and sculpted, or bulk up.

NUTRITION AND WEIGHT LOSS

No one person is identical and therefore everyone's nutritional needs will differ. You have probably read dozens, if not hundreds, of articles on blogs, websites, or in magazines that claim to have the one, true dietary solution to help you shed the pounds and keep them off. This does not hold true for everybody because of metabolic differences, hormones, health conditions, or straightforward genetics. So, what should you know and what should you do about your nutrition in conjunction with kettlebells that will help you lose weight?

‰ CRASH DIETS

Just don't do it. Crash diets have many detrimental side effects on your health and body. They deprive your body of vital nutrients and calories required for proper function. Severely restricting your calorie intake while training can lead to poor form, mistakes, and injuries. Most people also find that they pile all the weight back on right after they start eating normally again, which is extremely counterproductive to your efforts and does your confidence no good.

‰ "DIETS" AS A **LIFESTYLE**

There are many different ways of eating or lifestyle diets available that promise weight loss success. These diets may include banting, low-carb, high protein, the DASH diet, the Mediterranean diet, and many more. These diets are not your typical weight loss diet fads but rather a sustainable way of eating based on certain dietary principles. Some of them work for some people and not for others. If you are going to follow a new way of eating as prescribed by a specific lifestyle diet, do your research thoroughly beforehand and consult your medical practitioner for advice.

‰ HEALTHY AND **BALANCED**

The simplest way to combine sound nutrition and exercise for weight loss is to follow a healthy, balanced diet.

Eat a variety of different foods from all five main food groups: Fruit and vegetables, carbohydrates, protein, dairy, and healthy fats.

Divide your meal up into the food groups.

Fruits and vegetables should share a similar proportion of your meal as carbohydrates. These two food groups should be consumed daily and should form the largest part of your meal.

Proteins and pulses such as meat, dairy, fish, eggs, and legumes should form a smaller, moderate portion of your meal.

Healthy fats, while essential, should form only a small portion of your meal.

‰ PORTION CONTROL

It doesn't matter how healthy your diet is if you're eating too much of those healthy foods. Yes, you can eat too much healthy food. There is no single golden rule to follow about portion sizes. A slice of cake has more calories in it than a garden salad, even if the sizes of the servings are relatively similar. Adjust your portion sizes based on how many meals you eat per day and how many calories you need to take in. By dividing your daily caloric intake by the number of meals and snacks you have, you can get an idea of what your portion size should be per meal based on the calories in that portion.

‰ CALORIES COUNT

It doesn't matter how hard you train, if your calorie intake is equal to or higher than your calorie expenditure you won't lose weight. Weight loss follows a general rule of thumb: 80% diet and 20% exercise. While exercise is a vital part of overall health and weight management, your diet is a more important factor for successful weight loss.

Women need approximately 2000 calories a day to maintain their weight and lead a healthy lifestyle. This is a generalized figure and each person is different. For effective weight loss you need to approximate how many calories you, personally, need per day. Checking in with your physician or a dietitian can help you figure out how many calories your daily intake should be.

To lose weight, you must create a calorie deficit. By both watching what and how much you eat in relation to your daily calorie intake, you can successfully lose weight and keep it off.

‰ SUSTAINABILITY

The problem with going in a diet is that most diets that focus on weight loss offer bland foods, restrictive calorie intake, and tiny portion sizes. None of this is ultimately sustainable in the long run. If your diet is not sustainable as a lifestyle, you're going to pile the weight back on as soon as you go back to eating as you did before the diet. This is counterproductive and leads to yo-yo weight gain and weight loss.

To lose weight and keep it off, your diet needs to be a sustainable way of healthy eating that becomes a lifestyle instead of a short term quick fix. When considering whether a diet or way of eating is the right choice, ask yourself whether you can stick to that way of eating for the rest of your life. Another question to consider is whether you would recommend it to children. If the answer is no, then it's not going to stick and it would be better to find something else that will stick.

‰ DIETITIAN

If you are unsure about what you should be eating and how much in order to reach your weight loss goal, consult a qualified dietitian. A professional will help guide you through the best nutritional approach that is tailored to your health and body in order to reach your goals.

SCALE BACK THE OBSESSION

If there is one thing you should do with immediate effect is to stop obsessing over the scale. The scale can very easily turn into your worst enemy on your weight loss journey. Every scale has two sides to the story it tells you. It is telling you the truth. It is also telling you a blatant lie.

Your weight is a truth, whether you weigh 120 lbs or 200 lbs that is what you weigh. The lie is that your weight alone is not an indication of being overweight or not losing weight. This is especially important to keep in mind when you enter the world of kettlebells and strength training. When the result you are aiming for is weight loss, the scale is going to become a bone of contention.

You will not only be burning fat, but you will also be building lean muscle. Lean muscle weighs more than fat but it takes up less space. If you are losing fat but gaining muscle, the scale may deceive you into believing that you are not losing weight at all. This can be discouraging and could encourage negative thoughts to creep in.

Ditch the scale obsession and rely on other ways to track your weight loss when the scale stubbornly won't budge. Keep records of your shrinking measurements using a measuring tape or pay attention to how your clothes fit. As you burn fat and build muscle, your measurements will change and your clothes will fit better. There is no better affirmation of your weight loss than a shrinking waistline, not the number on the scale.

ONCE WEEKLY CHECK-INS

If you do weigh yourself, do so only once a week. Do it on the same day, at the same time, and with the same amount of clothing on (or naked). Don't change any of the variables and definitely do resist the temptation of hopping on the scale every day. The same applies to your measurements. Don't take them daily and follow the same rules of the same day, same time every week as with weighing yourself on the scale.

Our bodies undergo many fluctuations from one day to the next. Your body weight varies and your waist size may vary slightly at different times of the day and different days of the week. Being confronted with daily ups and downs can end up taking you on an emotional roller coaster ride that can derail your weight loss plan.

Chapter 6: Intermediate Exercises

Intermediate exercises are best done by people who have spent several beginner kettlebell sessions. Intermediate exercises are more physically challenging and may require more experience.

Kettlebell figure 8 targets

Targets: abdominals, back, arms

Stand with your legs slightly wider than your hip distance. Lower yourself in a squat position and remember to keep your back straight and your chest up. Hold one kettlebell with your left hand and swing it to your left leg then back between the legs. Pass the kettlebell in your right hand and swing it towards your right leg. This movement is similar to a classic basketball drill. Try to do as much repetitions in a minute.

Advanced kettlebell windmill

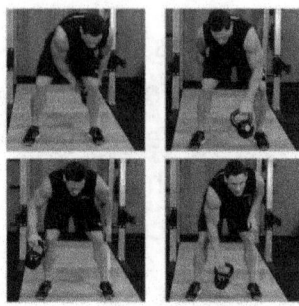

Targets: abdominals, hamstrings, shoulders, glutes

Press one kettlebell over your head with one arm. Keep the kettlebell locked out and push your butt into the direction of the kettlebell. Remember to keep the nonworking arm behind your back. Turn your feet 45 degrees from the arm holding the kettlebell. Lower your body and pause at the bottom. Reverse the motion into the starting position.

Kettlebell One leg Dead lift

Targets: Hamstrings, glutes, lower back

Hold the kettlebell with one hand. Lift the leg that is not on the same side as the hand that is holding the kettlebell. Keep your knees bent and perform a one legged dead lift by slightly bending your hips and extending your other leg behind for balance and support. Lower the kettlebell until it is parallel to the ground. Pause for a moment then return to the starting position.

One-arm kettlebell jerk

Targets: Shoulders, calves, triceps

Hold one kettlebell by the handle. Pull the kettlebell towards your shoulder by extending your arms through the legs and hips and placing the kettlebell at the back of your shoulder. Rotate your wrist with your palms facing forward.

Lower your body by bending your knees and keeping the torso upright. Quickly reverse the motion; you can jump to create momentum. As you jump, press the kettlebell overhead by extending your arms. Use your body to shift your weight. Return to a squat position while keeping the kettlebell overhead then return to a standing position. Lower your weight before doing another repetition.

Leg over floor press

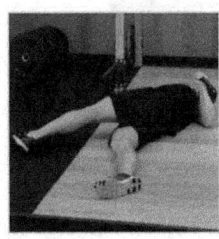 

Targets: chest, shoulders, triceps

Lie on the floor while holding one kettlebell in your chest. Extend one leg over the other leg. Extend your free arm to the side for support. Hold the kettlebell with your elbow lying flat on the floor. Extend you arm above your head then pause for a moment. Lower your elbow until it touches the ground. Remember to keep the kettlebell above your elbow. Repeat several times.

Alternating kettlebell row

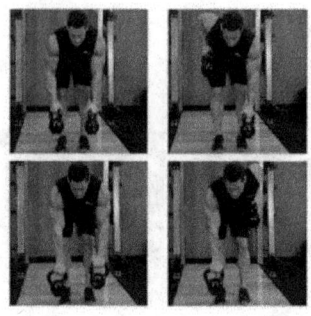

Targets: Middle back, biceps

Place two kettlebells in front of your feet. Bend slightly and push your butt out as much as possible. Bend over to grab both kettlebells by the handles. Lift one kettlebell while holding on to the other. Retract your shoulder blade as you flex your elbows. Draw the kettlebell towards your core. Slowly lower the kettlebell and repeat the motion with your other arm.

Kettlebell sumo high-pull

Targets: arm, back, shoulders

Stand with your feet apart. Place one kettlebell between your feet. Grab the kettlebell with both hands. Keep your knees bent and your hips back. Pull the kettlebell to your shoulders while you straighten your knees. Slowly extend your elbows. Remember that the force should be taken from the hips. Keep your core engaged the whole time. Bring the kettlebell down and repeat the movement.

Two Kettlebell Front Squat

Targets: legs back

Clean two kettlebells to your shoulders. Squat while pressing your heels into the ground and pushing your hips out. Make sure that your thighs are parallel to the ground. Return to the starting position and do another 15 repetitions.

Chapter 7: Workout Routine

Benefits to Switch up the Workout

In the recent time, it has been observed that monotony in the exercise routine is good for your health but may not give the desired result. As it is important to vary the exercises from time to time in order to achieve maximum fitness. In addition to this varied fitness, routine helps to stimulate different gig and small muscle groups. Currently, kettlebell training has proven to be the all-in-one workout of a lifetime, combining both strength and cardio aspects but it essential to try different exercises with it as well to gain more benefits. Moreover, it helps to prevent boredom by avoiding the same routine every day and encourage learning more techniques and exercises. Other than this, the benefits include:

Muscles Development: In case an individual follow the same routine of exercises every day then it may cause workout to become ineffective over a period. This is mainly because of two reasons; firstly, the muscles that are used to daily routine are exhausted which comparatively slow down the gains. Other than this, the muscles that are not used are neglected which may not produce the desired result. Therefore, it is important to change the workout routine to stimulate the body especially for people who are doing recreational exercisers. As professional sportsmen focus on particular exercise that builds very specific muscles according to their sport. Varied exercises help to a strong heart, muscular legs, and a powerful upper body. This can be achieved through prioritizing the work routine, for example, your monthly schedule can include weight lifting and aerobic exercises. This will help to build strength, flexibility and improve the stamina of the overall body simultaneously.

Weight-Loss: People who aim to lose weight often halt it as they follow the same routine every day, which makes the body used to it. Due to this, even after doing the same exercises and putting the same efforts, the person is unable to burn calories. Therefore, in order to resolve this issue, people should be encouraged to challenge the body with new exercises. It will force it to move in new ways and to begin from total inexperience again by allowing the body to do something new to adjust. Even though it requires more hard work but it will help to burn more calories during the workout. In addition to this, for people who want to lose weight, it is highly crucial to maintain a balanced diet and avoid food that may lead to weight gain

Prevent Injuries: It has been observed that repetitive exercises may increase the risk of causing several injuries such as strain injury. This is due to overuse of muscle groups, which make them exhausted to function efficiently. In order to avoid this, it is important to bring variety in exercises mainly because it gives an opportunity to work on new muscle groups and ligaments. On the other hand, overused muscles get time to recover and heal. Moreover, in case of injury, variety in exercise can help to perform a different activity that does not strain the same part of the body and will allow staying in shape and healing at the same time. For example, bodybuilders break up their workouts into individual muscle groups, which allow different muscles, joints, and ligaments to rest while avoiding stress on the body during the workout. In case, people continue to do the same exercise even after minor injury then it may lead to a severe problem that may take months to recover.

Prevent Boredom: There are high chances that an individual gets bored by following the same routine for the workout and may lose interest in it. As repetitive exercises may stress your body but do not help to achieve the desired result. In addition, without resistance, muscle exertion and an increased heart rate, the workout will be ineffective. For this purpose, it is important to keep the motivation level high by practicing new exercises in the workout routine and constantly trying new things. For example, a person who is into weight lifting only can enroll in Zumba class or anaerobic exercises. This will also help to explore more and depict which exercise is more suitable for the body. Moreover, when an individual starts a new routine, it helps to teach a new pattern, learning to think about how to improve and develop new moves. This will eventually encourage people not to skip the workout and keep the spirit high.

Healthy Brain: Exercises on regular basis helps to improve the brain function by preventing memory loss of an individual. Moreover, challenging and trying new exercises on daily basis helps the brain to develop new skills and keep neurons function efficiently. However, it is important to opt for right exercise in order to prevent any injury or overexertion. Research indicates that people who do not have a sedentary lifestyle and live an active life have fewer chances of diabetes, high cholesterol, hypertension and brain stroke.

Socializing: There is a sheer chance of meeting new people when an individual opts for different exercises for work out. This can also help to stay engaged with exercise, committed to a regular schedule of activity by finding people of your own interest and want to achieve the same goals. It can also motivate to try new exercises with others as well.

Improved Physique: People who tend to perform a variety of exercises during their work out are able to achieve fitness and are more physically strong. As exercise helps to build strong muscles and improve the functioning of the overall body. Therefore, it is highly recommended to try out new exercises with time depending on the potential of an individual.

How to Change Workout Routine

As discussed above it is essential to change the workout routine by introducing new exercises with time. However, in order to avoid any negative impact on the body, it is important to do a thorough study or consult a trainer before opting for a new exercise. In addition to this, it is suggested to try anything new from basic level for example, if an individual spends 30 minutes on a stationary bike, then he can increase the intensity of the workout by adding speed, or by spending 10 out of the 30 minutes on a treadmill.

Moreover, there are various signs, which indicate that an individual needs to change their exercise routine, which most commonly include that the person despite maintaining a balanced diet is unable to identify any physical difference in the body. This depicts that there is a need to try new exercises, which may prove to be beneficial for the body. In addition to this, if an individual is not feeling hungry after a good workout then it is crucial to make amendments in the exercises. As during workout, the body is repairing the muscle fiber that gets broken down during the workout. It needs protein and nutrients to generate new muscle protein strand hence the reason an individual feel hungry after a good workout. Whereas, if the workouts are easy, then there are no muscle fibers to repair and the body does not require additional food.

Chapter 8: Full Body Or Holistic Exercises

These exercises are what the kettlebell was built for. Most of these exercises involve body movements that we make every day, or that are vital to the proper fitness and flexibility of our bodies. For that reason, most of these exercises should be approached with some form of caution as having the wrong form or posture while doing these can inevitably lead to one form of injury or another. When done in the right manner though, these can be some of the most fun workout routines you will ever encounter in your life.

1. Russian Kettlebell Swing

Target muscle group: Shoulders, Back, Hips, Glutes, Legs

Walkthrough: This is one of the easiest, most basic Kettlebell exercises to do, yet also one of the most taxing. The Russian

Kettlebell swing is easy to learn, easy to perfect and works out the whole body from head to toe. To successfully complete this maneuver, stand straight with your feet hip distance apart and grab the handle of a kettlebell, keeping your pals facing down, and your arms straight. Bend your knees slightly and drive your hips back, lowering your body marginally (not all the way like you would with a squat). Swing the kettlebell forward while straightening your legs and your hips as you go. Lower the weight back between your legs to complete one rep.

With this exercise, it is important to note that the main movement comes from the hips, not the arms, as you return to an upright position. If done properly, this exercise should engage mainly your glutes, lower back, core, arms, shoulders and of course, your hips. This exercise can be done one or two handed. If done with one hand, alternate hands every time the kettlebell ends up in the start position (between your legs), and remember to keep your free arm swinging to the rhythm to help maintain momentum.

2. The Sidestep Kettlebell Swing

Target muscle group: Legs, Glutes and Back, Shoulders

Walkthrough: This exercise is a variation of the routine detailed above, and has shown that it is not only a welcome addition to any routine, but that as there is a lot of added movement to it, it adds a different dynamic that most find almost exciting. Most people agree that adding this variation to the kettlebell swing to your workout will help to kill the ordinary nature of your workout, and will help bring some sort of excitement back into the workout environment

For this exercise, you will need to grab the kettlebell and start with the basic kettlebell swing described above. When the kettlebell is between your feet, sidestep right with your right foot. When the bell is at its peak in the air, bring your left foot up to meet the right foot. Keep sidestepping in this manner for the desired number of reps. At the end of the set, repeat the exercise, but side step in the opposite direction.

As part of a set this is a brilliant exercise to try out, but why not challenge yourself and see just how long you can sidestep before you give up. This will help you gauge whether you are on track to hit your target fitness level or whether you still have work to do.

3. The Kettlebell Lunge press

Target muscle group: Shoulders, Back, Arms, Abs, Glutes, Legs

Walkthrough: Traditional lunges call for a very simple, straightforward set of movements to achieve their goal. This workout promises to be an interesting twist to the traditional lunge, and is sure to add an extra bit of spice to your workout. On top of targeting both your glutes and your legs as with the traditional lunges, it also helps build your shoulders, arms and back when the press is added to complete a truly full body exercise.

As with a normal lunge, you start off by standing straight, holding the kettlebell in one hand at chest level, with your arm bent and your palm facing inwards. Lunge forward with one leg, while raising the kettlebell above your head. Return to the starting position and count the whole movement as one rep. After a particular number of reps, switch hands and legs and repeat the process to complete one set.

This exercise is a must for those who are looking to build up strength in their legs and in their glutes, and is also very effective for those willing to improve the strength and flexibility of their shoulders.

4. The Kettlebell Sumo High pull

Target muscle group: Arms, Shoulders, Legs, Back

Walkthrough: This is a fluid exercise that can be used to increase back strength, especially in the lower back, and is very effective in helping to create power and stamina in your legs. It is also quite effective in building up the strength of your arms and shoulders.

To perform this exercise, first stand with the kettlebell between your feet, keeping your feet just a bit wider than shoulder length apart. Bend down into an almost squatting position, bending the knees slightly and pushing your hips back, remembering to keep your back straight. Grip the kettlebell with both hands and pull it up to chin or shoulder height as you straighten up your legs and hips. Return the weight back to the ground or between your feet to complete one rep.

Remember, the driving force behind this exercise as with most exercises that adopt a similar position, are your hips. Though the arms also play a small role, this only comes in with the pulling at the very end, when the kettlebell has to come up to shoulder level. Even though they play a minor role, the benefits to your arms and shoulders after a few sets of the Sumo High Pull will not go unnoticed.

Chapter 9: Kettlebell Exercises

Kettlebell Goblet Squat

The kettlebell goblet squat is a lower body exercise that develops strength of quadriceps femoris muscles and calf muscles. Unlike the traditional squats, it is done by keeping the body in an erect position that results in lesser strain on the spine and lower lumbar. Holding the kettlebell in front shifts your center of gravity, which tightens up your trunk and abs in order to brace the weight.

The Kettlebell Goblet Squat can be done in two ways. One way is using a heavier kettlebell with fewer repetitions that causes tears in the muscle fiber and cause them to grow thicker and stronger. Another method involves high work rate with low repetitions forcing more and more oxygenated blood into the hamstrings, quadriceps, and glutes.

The goblet squat can be performed using dumbbells, medicine balls, sandbags, and other free weights, but the kettlebell is perfectly designed for the goblet squat because it shifts your center of gravity allowing you to exert more force. Also, kettlebells come with handles so you can hold it nice and contained against your chest.

How to do a Kettlebell Goblet Squat

Stand up straight holding the kettlebell by its handle at your chest height.

Slowly descend into a squat position keeping your head and chest up and maintaining your back in a straight position until your hamstrings are touching your calves.

Pause briefly at this position and then move upwards concentrating the force on your legs and not on your back.

Tips to Perform Kettlebell Goblet Squat Correctly

Throughout the movement, the kettlebell and your arms should not move and all the movement should come from your legs. Keep your back straight and your abs locked, do not arch your back or bend forward. Your elbows should remain between your knees. Heels and toes should remain planted on the floor and the hips should ascend at the same rate as the shoulders. Never perform kettlebell goblet squat in bare feet because in case the kettlebell is dropped it can cause fractures.

Video: https://youtu.be/mvVPrpusmrk

Kettlebell Squat

Kettlebell squat is the most basic exercise to familiarize an individual with kettlebell training. Squat is a basic human movement, which is used often in everyday tasks such as sitting in a chair. Squat is an essential for kettlebell training. Regular squats improve posture, mobility, and strengthen the lower body.

Holding a kettlebell while doing squats can target your arms, shoulders, and abs muscles. Kettlebell squats are great for weight loss and strength building. This exercise is designed to mobilize your large muscle groups, which include quadriceps, glutes, and hamstrings. Kettlebell squats are also called Kettlebell front squats because weight is in front of you unlike traditional squats in which force is exerted across your shoulders.

How to do a Kettlebell Squat

Stand tall with your feet shoulder-width apart and toes pointed outwards and hold the base of the kettlebell in both hands with palms facing each other.

Bend elbows and bring kettlebell up to the chest level with its handle facing you.

Squat downwards by bending both knees 90 degrees until your thighs are parallel with the floor and your hips drop below knees.

Stand back up and push hips forward as you stand up.

Squat downwards immediately.

Tips to Perform Kettlebell Squat Correctly

Keep the kettlebell stable through the movement in front of your chest. Avoid bending the back and shoulders. Stand tall and do not let the knees bend inward.

Video: https://youtu.be/LNsI2Ugcu9s

Kettlebell Deadlift

Kettlebell Deadlift is a frightening name of an extremely functional kettlebell exercise that utilizes every muscle in your body, burns more calories, builds strength, increases flexibility and turn on your nervous system all at once. It strengthens the muscles of your back, hips, glutes, and hamstrings.

Like kettlebell squats, the kettlebell deadlift is one of the fundamental daily human movements. It is basically the action of lifting a weight off the ground. So, whenever you scoop up your kid in your arms or lift a box off the floor, you are basically performing a deadlift.

How to do a Kettlebell Deadlift

Stand with your feet shoulder-width apart and a kettlebell placed in-between your legs.

Bend knees, tighten your lower back, and lower down to pick up the kettlebell.

Keep your hips back and your knees behind the toes.

Pick up the kettlebell and stand up using the power of your legs.

Tips to Perform Kettlebell Deadlift

In order to perform a kettlebell deadlift correctly you should keep your back flat, your hips above your knees, and your shins vertical.

Video: https://youtu.be/zF5CGQmNxyI

Variations of Kettlebell Deadlift

There are three variations of kettlebell deadlifts: single leg deadlift using single weight, single leg deadlift using two weights, and deadlift to squat thrust.

Single Leg Deadlift Using Single Weight

This variation of kettlebell deadlift is recommended for beginners. It is done using one kettlebell only. Using two kettlebells in the beginning of kettlebell training can lead to injury due to overextension. It is important to select an appropriate size of kettlebell to properly impact on your muscles.

Single Leg Deadlift Using Two Weights

Kettlebell deadlift with two weights is recommended for advanced lifters who have build enough strength after practicing kettlebell deadlifts with single weight.

Deadlift to Squat Thrust

This is one of the most intensive kettlebell exercises. It is a combination of kettlebell deadlift and squat thrust. It is done by bending downwards to the floor with a kettlebell in each hand. The legs are then moved forward in a single motion and the movement is finished off with a normal kettlebell deadlift.

Kettlebell Swing

Kettlebell swings are great full-body exercises for beginners that are designed to build strength and improve posture. The kettlebell swing is the basic of all ballistic kettlebell exercises. It is one of the most metabolic exercises that results in rapid calories burn and weight loss. It also increases strength of the shoulders and lower back.

Kettlebell swings are best for individuals who have back pain or other problems because of sedentary lifestyle. They are also very helpful in maintaining cardiovascular fitness. A study conducted by the U.S. Truman State University showed that traditional kettlebell swing is a more effective cardio workout than other traditional weight training circuits.

The kettlebell swing is one of the basic kettlebell exercises, which trains a beginner to perform hip hinges that are essential to perform advanced kettlebell exercises such as kettlebell deadlifts and all bent over rows.

How to do a Kettlebell Swing

Stand with your feet shoulder-length apart and hold a kettlebell with both hands.

Slightly bend your knees while keeping your chest lifted.

Push your hips backward and hinge your torso until it is parallel with the floor.

Extend your arms and allow the kettlebell to drop between your legs.

Squeeze your glutes and push hips forward

Propel the kettlebell to shoulder-height and allow it to swing back down.

Tips to Perform a Kettlebell Swing Correctly

Make sure that your feet are planted firmly on the floor and shoulders are connected to the body. There should be no forward knee movement on the upswing and spine should be neutral. The back should be flat to avoid any injury.

Video: https://youtu.be/q0jalJ-3e7U

Kettlebell One-Handed Swing

Single-arm or one-handed kettlebell swing is a more intensive variation of the traditional kettlebell swing. It works the same way as the two-handed swing but is much more demanding on your whole body. It helps in developing a stronger midline and a stronger lower back through stabilization and activation of the core muscles. It strengthens the hamstrings and glutes. Kettlebell one-handed swing also improves cardiovascular endurance.

Kettlebell one-handed swing is performed the same way as the traditional kettlebell swing. The obvious difference is that it is performed with one hand instead of two.

How to do a Kettlebell One-Handed Swing

Place the kettlebell in front of you on the ground, settled in between your legs.

Stand straight with your head up, hips back, chest open, and weight on your heels.

Grasp the kettlebell with one hand and simultaneously extend your legs and pull the kettlebell up.

Your goal is to project the kettlebell to your chest level. It is normal to take few repetitions to get it to your chest or eye level.

Perform five to ten repetitions and then place the kettlebell back on the ground. Switch hands and perform kettlebell swings for five to ten times again.

You can also attempt to do single-handed kettlebell swing with hand switch. The key in this movement is timing. Switch the kettlebell from one hand to another when it is at the top end of the swing.

Tips for Performing One-Handed Kettlebell Swings Correctly

The most important consideration in a kettlebell swing is your spine position. Any sort of flexion can be dangerous and cause injuries. Apply force only when extending your hips and legs. Too much tension throughout the whole movement can reduce the efficiency and power of the exercise.

Video: https://youtu.be/9W7ZiimlfaE

Chapter 10: Work Outs

When you are new to kettlebell work outs or you are currently out of shape and you want to ease out into routine work out slowly its necessary to start out slow with the basics. There is no need to go to complex intense movements when you are still learning and increasing your body conditioning. Start slowly and move on when you feel you need additional challenge. When planning your work out regime don't forget the legs. You can work on the legs by doing the kettlebell suitcase squats or kettlebell lunges. Suitcase squats are easier and simple because they require no skill but you will need two bells. When doing the lunges you will need to rack the kettlebell in the crook of your arm giving you the perfect excuse to learn how to do the kettlebell clean

Kettlebell exercises are space saving compared to other exercises like the treadmill or even a gym. Unlike other weights and techniques kettlebells variations and techniques are just endless. The workouts are not meant for men only but can also be done by women. Women who complain of trouble trying control weight loss because of slow metabolism can undertake kettlebell swings to shed those unwanted pounds.

Kettlebell swing ids the fundamental exercise as the movement is the foundation upon which most beginners work outs are built. They build up you muscle endurance while gently easing your body into an exercise habit. Including swings in your workout routine makes you strong and fit to move on to more complex and demanding kettlebell moves.

Exercises involving the upper body can be divided into two i.e. push and pull. By pushing you work your body on the chest shoulders and triceps and by pulling you work your upper back and biceps. Failure to include push and pull in your work out leads to unbalance and may lead to injuries.

CORE WORK OUTS

This workout exercises your whole body. The core mostly feels the burn when you done. The exercises are perfect in that they improve core strength by enhancing the strength and flexibility of all related muscles extending outwards to the extremities. The shape and movement of the kettlebells at the end of your arms keeps you off balance and more muscles are required to stabilize your body. The fact that the kettlebell is not stationary in your hands adds to the dynamics of each movement, forcing muscles to compensate for the changing centre of gravity.

KETTLEBELL ARMS

To completely work out the arms one needs to work out all the muscle groups which include the biceps triceps and forearm. Depending on the intended aim one can use heavy weights to build muscle and strength with lower reps or can do more exercises with more repetitions when burning fats is the aim

KETTLEBELL PRESS

The kettlebell press or overhead press is a wonderful strength building lift for all pressing needs. It is unlike a normal dumbbell press or dumbbell because of the offset nature of the kettlebell. If it's your first time then you in for a big surprise. The awkward shape of the kettlebell makes it handling a little more complex as it requires the participant have some technique if he is to handle it with some degree of control. By having the weight rest against the back of your arm it tries to pull you out of your groove and into a somehow dangerous position. One needs to learn how to clean and rack the bell first and then follow it up with pressing. Clean and racks are a prerequisite position before executing the military press or other lifts. A solid and consistent clean makes the press successful. It does not matter how strong you are if your clean delivers the weight to a poor rack then the pres will be a struggle. Breath is an important aspect of creating tension and relaxation. Prepare your body for the impact which should be minimal.

How it's done

This part of the lift essentially gets the bell to a racked position at your chest with your arm at rest against your body. Your fist should be below your chin and your legs locked out feet set slightly wider than shoulder width distance apart in length. To hold the bell correctly at the rack, you will have to lock your hips and knees by clenching your glutes and tightening your quads.

Execution

Clean a kettlebell to your shoulder by extending through the legs and hip as you pull the kettlebell towards your shoulder. As you doing that rotate your wrist so that your palm faces inward. This is the starting position.

Look at the kettlebell as you press it up and out overhead.

Slowly lower the kettlebell to your shoulders and repeat. For maximum stability ensure you contact your lat butt and stomach.

When in this position you will be forcing your hips forward creating space for your arms to rest against your body while the bell is on the rack.

KETTLEBELL SWING

This is a classic kettlebell movement and is perfect for beginners. It is a fundamental movement for a great group of kettlebell movements. The muscles targeted include hips, legs, glutes, back and shoulders. The swing utilizes a hip thrust important to other movements such as the one arm snatch. To develop maximum fitness strength and endurance levels one needs to learn effective and efficient swing techniques.

You need to find a kettlebell you can confidently swing and place it on the floor between your feet. Start with the kettlebell slightly in front of you positioned between your legs which should be wider than shoulder width. Look straight ahead and keep your neck in a neutral position with your knees slightly bent, your back flat and hip pointing backwards. Do not go too low as this should be between a squat and a stand. Hike the kettlebell behind you like in American football but keep hold of the kettlebell stretching the hamstrings. Count to three in your head and then fluidly and in one continuous motion extend your hips forcefully and extend the kettlebell along its arc till it reaches about the chest length. Contract your abs and glutes for stability. In this movement your arms act as just a hook and the power originates from movement of the hips and the posterior chain i.e. glutes lower back and hamstrings. This movement should be fluid with no rest in between reps. the important part in this exercise is to work with the swinging motion rather than against it.

Swinging the kettlebells higher than chest height is not efficient and there's little to be gained. You breathe out at the apex of the swing. You can target your abs by focusing on tilting your pelvis up at the top of the swing.

As you let the kettlebell fall free back between your legs breathe in hold your breath. The hips should move backwards to allow loading of the posterior chain to enable power for the subsequent swing.

Single arm kettlebell swing

This works in the same way as a Russian kettlebell but now in unilateral fashion. You alternate the arms in between sets.

Execution

The starting position is similar to that of the Russian kettlebell swing. You need to stand straight with your feet shoulder width apart and keeping your neck in a neutral position. With the kettlebell handle in one hand and the other hand free to swing and drive momentum, bend your knees slightly lowering your body to the ground and driving your hips backwards. Explode upwards moving your hips forwards and contracting your abs and glutes for stability. Swing the kettlebell until your arms is parallel to the floor. Your other arm swings to aid in momentum. Lower the kettlebell to the staring position. Do not switch the arms between each rep but rather wait till the end to ensure muscles work to their full potential.

One arm kettlebell swing

This is a great movement as it engages the back and legs. It takes some time to get it right so one should take it slow in the beginning. The muscles involved include the back, legs, glutes and core.

Execution

Start with legs shoulder width apart and place the kettlebell between your feet. Hold the kettlebell in one hand with a loose grip and your thumb pointing behind you to prevent the kettlebell from hitting your wrist. Pull the bell up to your shoulder level and in the process exhale and tense the muscles in your core and glutes. The aim is to keep the kettlebell close to your body at all times. Refrain from swinging the arm not lifting the bell at all times and keep it tight. In a slow but controlled motion return the kettlebell back to the starting position. Do not switch arms between reps but swap between sets instead. It is also important to engage your core at the top of the movement.

Kettlebell deadlift

This is the king of all leg movements. The muscles targeted include legs arms back core and glutes.

Execution

In this routine stand with your legs a little closer than your shoulder width and place the kettlebell in between your legs. Squat down and hold the kettlebell with both hands in such a way that your knuckles point in front of you. Your knees and hip should be bent and your back flat. Tighten your arms and keep them extended while engaging your core and glutes. Slowly stand up driving your hips upwards and pause at the top to squeeze before reversing the movement and putting the kettlebell to the starting postion. Don't overextend and roll backwards. The reps should be smooth instead of a fast one.

KETTLEBELL ARM WORK OUT

When using kettlebells to work on arms, the shape and grip will influence the target muscle. You can target your triceps and biceps differently. Depending on the aim of the work out you can use heavier weights in case you want to build muscles and strength with lower reps or you can do more exercises with more repetitions if you want to burn some calories. A complete training should work on all the groups of muscles which are biceps triceps and forearm.

KETTLEBELL ROWS

This is a wonderful variation from the traditional bent over row. This exercise primarily works on the muscles of the back. It also works on the legs core and hips. There are different ways of doing it but in all the variations you should always push your butt behind you as much as possible to begin the movement.

ONE ARM KETTELBELL

By making a staggered stance the kettlebell will go next to your front foot.

Move the elbow up towards the ceiling. The elbow should be close to the body. Slowly bring the bell up to near your stomach.

TWO ARM KETTLEBELL ROW

This movement is great for working the back and shoulders. It depends on a straight Back and tight core. The muscles targeted are arms back and shoulders.

Execution

Stand with feet at shoulder width apart and place a kettlebell in front of each foot. While keeping your back flat and your neck in a neutral position slightly bend at the knees. Grab both kettlebells and pull them towards your stomach while still avoiding standing up or moving your knees and back. The movement resembles that of a rowing machine with your elbows moving backwards. The movement in both arms should be equal to each other. This move should be fluid while also keeping the elbows close to the body. Tense your core at the top of the rep and keep everything tight then slowly lower the weights in a controlled motion back to the starting position.

The renegade alternating kettlebell

This variation incorporates a whole lot of additional muscle groups. You assume a push up position and hold each kettlebell with one hand. You then shift the weight to one kettlebell while you do a row with the other.

KETTLEBELL RUSSIAN TWIST

This is one of the most effective methods of building a strong and defined abs and core strength. The muscles targeted are the abs and oblique's.

Execution

The starting position looks similar to that of a crunch but now with the legs about a hip apart. With your feet flat on the ground sit with the legs bent at the knees. With both hands pick up the kettlebell and bring it to your chest. Lean back a little bit to make a 45- degree angle. Now twist your torso from left to right starting at the waist. Do not swing the weight but rather pick it from your left side and bring it over your body and place it on the other side and then repeat. Always ensure you keep the movement in control.

KETTLEBELL SQUAT

Kettlebell squat is a superior exercise for an average person who doesn't have good flexibility mobility and core strength. Placing the weight in front of the body makes it easier on the spine and knees making it easier to stay in the best position as compared to traditional barbell back squat.

Execution

Sit back like you are seated in a chair, adjust you back to stay flat as your spine is lengthened and chest stays tall. The foot position should be narrower stance than normal mostly between shoulder and hip width apart. Perfect the move before plunging into your regular workouts. The work out is done at the beginning of your routine with sub maximal weight to achieve a nice warm up. This exercise is superior to other forms of squat so take your time to learn the move properly and you will be glad you did it.

This workout takes it easy on you with only two different exercises. Make sure you pick a kettlebell that you can handle comfortably. Do each exercise for 50-40-30-20-10 reps.

KETTLEBELL SNATCH

This combines the kettlebell press and swing. It is referred to as the czar by some Russians. It is vital in building a superior core with hip power and shoulder strength to produce unbelievable power. To perform the snatch you need first to have learnt to do the swing so that you know your arc of swing. The key is to know your shoulder mobility and flexibility before you can progress to trying the snatch. You start with the kettlebell in between your legs. You swing it all the way back and then swing it back all the way so that your arm is directly above your head. The repeated swings up and down will burn off some calories and build the muscles affected by the press and swing target. Ensure the bell does not bhang your arm when performing this as that would mean you either using too much weight, your technique is poor or the arc of your swing is too wide. Apart from posterior chain conditioning the snatch is also a brilliant exercise for the shoulder girdle. For this move you need to quickly decentralize and stabilize the kettlebell and this builds incredible strength and stability. For many persons with weak posterior muscles and conditioning the snatch acts as powerful remedy with a powerful hip hinge. The overhead position has to be stable with no deviation. This is important in developing shoulder stability.

Another great benefit of snatch is that it can be great alternative to the overhead press if you have shoulder issues particularly if you have been working out with barbell press. Kettlebell snatch is magnificent in developing aerobic capacity. It is impactful as compared to many other activities and has impressive metabolic response making it an alternative to traditional aerobic activities.

Since the kettlebell snatch strengthens stabilizes and builds the aerobic capacity it is referred to as the mother of all kettlebell exercises due to the multitude of benefits it brings.

KETTLEBELL LUNGES

The muscles targeted are the quadriceps, glutes, hamstrings and calf muscles. The core is activated due to the unilateral movement required of this exercise. The kettlebells are held for an extended period of time to help build forearms and traps. Lunges are useful for sports requiring frequent lunging activities eg tennis badminton fencing and even soccer and basketball.

Execution

Step forward with your right foot and assume a lunge position. When in this position pass the kettlebell through your legs to your other hand and then stand up straight. Step forward with your left foot and repeat the steps again as many times as needed.

Backward stepping lunge is one of the easiest methods to learn the lunge and get used to the balance. It allows you to control the pressure on your knees completely hence good for those with tricky knees.

KETTLEBELL HIGH PULL

This exercise works on the upper body. The movement starts at the heels rising through the hips. The muscles targeted are the arms, shoulders, traps, legs and glutes.

Execution

You start the exercise by standing a little bit wider than shoulder width apart and the feet angled at 45 degrees. The kettlebell should start on the ground between you legs. While keeping your core tight squat down and take the kettlebell handle in one hand. Move up with your hips and push your heels into the ground. Move into a standing position while at the same time pulling the kettlebells upwards. The elbows drive the kettlebells upwards and once at the top hold momentarily before going back to the starting position. During this execise ensure your chest is high and your core is tight throughout the movement. This aids in stability and control. The kettlebell should start on the ground and return there after every complete rep.

Chapter 11: Ways To Use Kettlebells

There are three major ways in which you can use kettlebells when working out. These include:

1. Warm-ups

Kettlebells are the best tools to avoid imbalances and injuries. This is mainly because they will warm up your body by simply restoring healthy movement patterns in your body.

However, if you are not ready to start integrating kettlebells in your workout program, at least start using them little by little to enhance your mobility. This will help you get in position so that you can perform regular exercise movements safely. So when you lift heavier, your body can handle it and you can maintain the technique.

Even though the kettlebells are much lighter than you think or what you are used to, they offer you adequate feedback to challenge yourself and engage your nervous system. This means

that the communication between the body and the brain is enhanced and this boosts a more responsive system to what you are asking it to do.

The trick here is to first master the goblet squats before you can proceed to back squats by simply holding the lower position for a couple of seconds before opening up the hips. You can also try doing the light one-arm overhead presses before progressing to military presses so that your shoulders stay warm. Alternatively, you can use choose to use the chest-loaded swings to make your hips ready for kettlebell deadlifts.

2. Doing Full Body Workouts

All that you need for a great workout is to ensure that you are working all the major and minor muscles of your body. With kettlebells, you can achieve this using squats, hinge, pull and push techniques.

Once you cover these movement patterns, you are good to go.

3. Set A Circuit

When it comes to swings and getups, you will get your heart rate up the same way you would in a cardio machine. The most important thing with the kettlebell is that you can do more to re- enforce good mechanics. The other bright side is that while you exercise, you are challenging yourself to be better while having so much fun. The trick here is to build a circuit with kettlebells before you progress to heavy weight-training sessions.

Chapter 12: Kettlebell Goblet Squat

The Kettlebell goblet squat is the king of all kettlebell leg exercises. Start of light and feel the burn!

Muscles Targeted: Legs, Back, Abs and Glutes

Method:

Take a kettlebell in both hands and hold it out in front of your chest. Keep your back straight and look straight ahead. Keep your elbows close to your body and the kettlebell close but not resting on your chest. Slowly start squatting. Push your hips backwards, until your thighs are parallel to the ground and drive your heals into the ground. Keep your core tight to aid stability and keep your back and neck straight. Get down into a full squatting position (no half squats allowed!) and then hold the position momentarily. Then drive your hips upwards and return to the starting position.

Video: https://www.youtube.com/watch?v=9TOlFFKzWO0

Top Tips:

-Take it slow and focus on good form

-Keep your core tight, the whole exercise.

-Focus on your breathing to aid the rhythm of the movement.

Kettlebell Figure of Eight

The kettlebell figure of eight is a complicated movement, but once you have mastered the hand over, it will become one of your favorite exercises.

Muscles Targeted: Abs, Obliques, Arms and back

Method:

Start by standing with your legs shoulder width apart and lower down into a quarter-squat. Take the kettlebell in your left hand and swing it around your left leg and then bring it back between your legs. Pass the kettlebell into your right hand

and then bring it around the outside of your right legs and back round in between your legs. Continue passing the kettlebell between hands and then between your legs in a figure of eight motion. Keep this movement going for 30 seconds and then switch directions.

Video: https://www.youtube.com/watch?v=bAlHvT1tH5Y

Top Tips

-Focus on the movement of the kettlebell, think 'figure of eight' or imagine the age-old basketball drill.

-Start off slowly, until you have mastered the switch over between hands.

-Keep your back flat the whole time and keep your core tight to aid stability.

-You may need to experiment with how low you squat, this is different for everybody based on the length of their arms/legs and their height.

Kettlebell Lunge Press

The kettlebell Lunge press is a great full body movement that works all major muscle groups.

Muscles targeted: Shoulders, Arms, Back, Glutes, Legs Abs and Obliques

Method:

Start the movement by standing up straight with your knees in a neutral position (don't lock your legs) and the kettlebell in front of your chest in one hand (the hand on the side that you are going to lunge from i.e. right hand if right leg lunges out in front of you and vice versa). The arm holding the kettlebell should be bent. Step forward and lunge with one leg while simultaneously raising the kettlebell above your head. Hold the position at the top and then return to the starting position. Repeat the motion on the same side until you have finished your set and then repeat with the opposite leg.

Video: https://www.youtube.com/watch?v=eCl0sHxzY9E

Top Tips:

-Keep your core tight to aid stability.

-Keep your neck in a neutral position and don't crane your neck to look at the kettlebell when it is overhead.

-Focus on your breathing to help aid the movement and maintain control

Kettlebell high pull

The Kettlebell high pull is a great exercise for working the upper body, it is an explosive movement that starts at the heels and rises through the hips.

Muscles Targeted: Arms, Shoulders, Traps, Legs and Glutes

Method:

Stand a bit wider then shoulder width apart and angle your feet outwards at a 45-degree angle. The kettlebell should start on the ground between your legs.

Squat down while keeping your core tight and take the kettlebell handle in one hand. Drive up with your hips and push your heels into the ground. Explode into a standing position while pulling the kettlebell upwards. The elbows should drive the kettlebell upwards. Visualize the weight rising up in a straight line perpendicular to the floor. Once you have reached the top of the rep, hold momentarily before returning the kettlebell to the ground and starting another rep.

Video: https://www.youtube.com/watch?v=Li4g5p6s2eM

Top Tips:

-Keep your chest high

-Keep your core tight throughout the movement to aid stability and control.

-The kettlebell should start on the ground and return there after every rep.

Kettlebell push ups

Kettlebell Push ups are a great way of showing you the diverse nature of exercises you can do with kettlebells.

Muscles Targeted: Biceps, Triceps, Chest Abs and Back

Method:

This movement is essential a simple push up but it is done on kettlebells. This will increase the stress on your abs and it is therefore important to keep your core tight and back flat. Start by grabbing hold of the kettlebell handles and rest in a plank with your arms locked. Then bend your elbows and go down into a deep press up. Hold the position at the bottom of the rep before exploding back upwards and pushing down to return to the starting position. This is much harder then it looks and certainly harder then standard press ups.

Video: https://www.youtube.com/watch?v=GHvCLvOGOHs

Top Tips:

-Focus on your breathing and breathe at the top and bottom of each rep

-Keep that core tight to make it easier to balance in the starting plank position.

Weekly routine

For best results, it is a good idea to split your workouts into groups and work on different muscle groups and at different weights.

For example,

2 days a week you do a full body workout with lighter weights and high reps to focus on aerobic fitness and fat loss.

2 days a week you may do low reps of heavy weights to build strength, perhaps with one day focusing on lower body and one day on upper body.

2 days a week you might do medium amount of reps with a moderate weight to work on building muscle, again split into

one day of lower body and one day of upper body.

Finally, you might choose to do an abs work out, focusing on really working the core and building those abs.

Or more simply:

Monday – Heavy upper body (building strength)

Tuesday – Light, high intensity (fat loss)

Wednesday – Medium lower body (hypertrophy – building muscle)

Thursday – Rest

Friday - Heavy lower body

Saturday – Light, high intensity (fat loss)

Sunday – Medium upper body (hypertrophy – building muscle)

With a separate abs work out on Mondays, Wednesdays and Saturdays.

As the weeks progress, you can add in more hypertrophy exercises and more light, high intensity exercises to improve results.

Conclusion

Thank you for buying this book. I hope that it has helped you learn how to start training with kettlebells to achieve that shredded body you've always wanted. But more than just learning, I'd like to encourage you to start applying what you learned as soon as possible because learning or knowing is just half the battle for a shredded body. The other half is action or application of knowledge. And the longer you put off applying what you learned, the higher your risks of not using kettlebells to train and, consequently, increase the chances of not being able to achieve that body you've always dreamed of.

www.ingramcontent.com/pod-product-compliance
Lightning Source LLC
LaVergne TN
LVHW011958070526
838202LV00054B/4957